Piano • Vocal • Guitar

backStreetboys never gone

Cover photo by Yuri Elizondo

ISBN 1-423-40444-0

7777 W. BLUEMOUND RD. P.O. BOX 13819 MILWAUKEE, WI 53213

Visit Hal Leonard Online at
www.halleonard.com

INCOMPLETE

Words and Music by LINDY ROBBINS,
DAN MUCKALA and JESS CATES

*Recorded a half step lower.

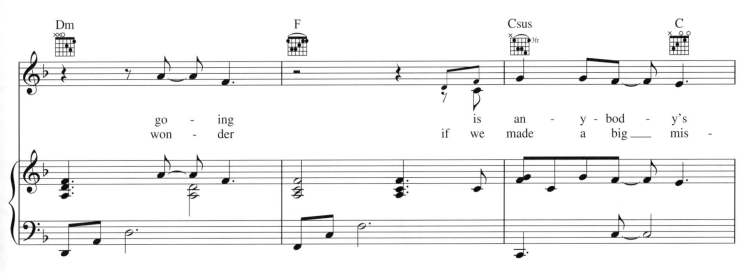

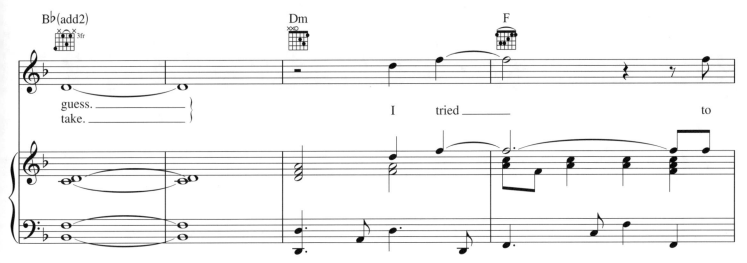

go on like ___ I nev - er knew ___ you. I'm a - wake ___

___ but my world is half ___ a - sleep. ___

I pray ___ for this heart to be ___ un - bro -

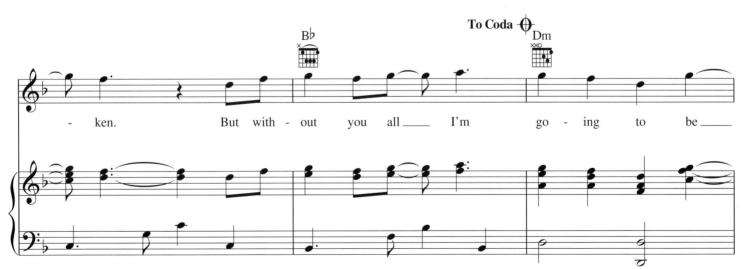

- ken. But with - out you all ___ I'm go - ing to be ___

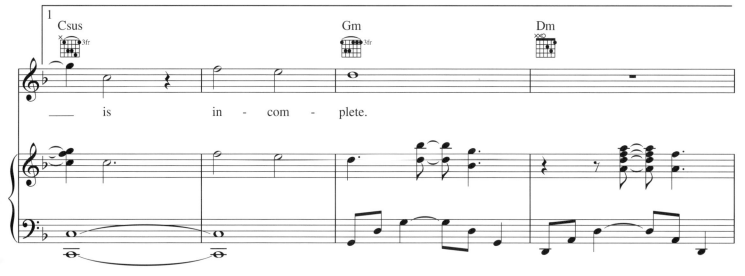

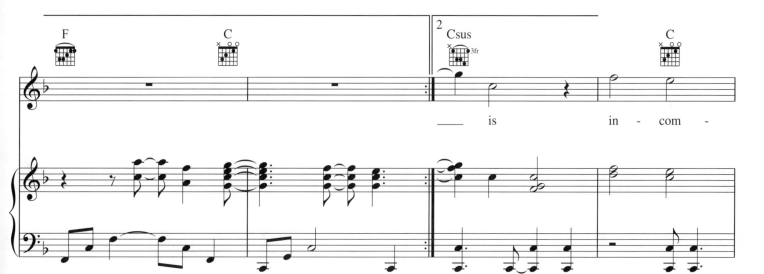

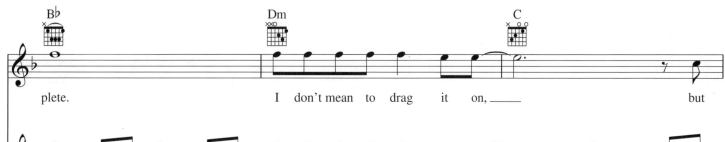

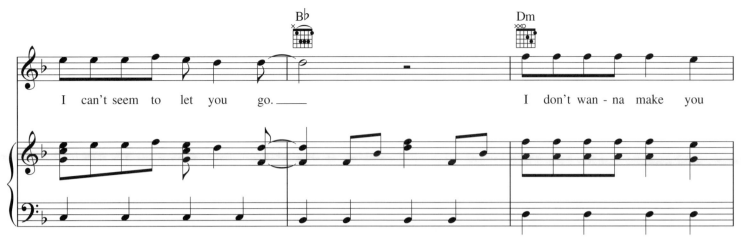

I can't seem to let you go. _____ I don't wan - na make you

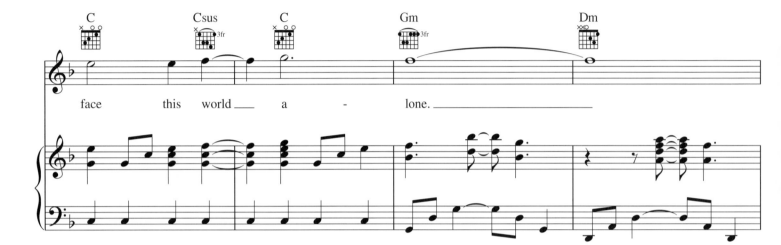

face this world ___ a - lone. _____

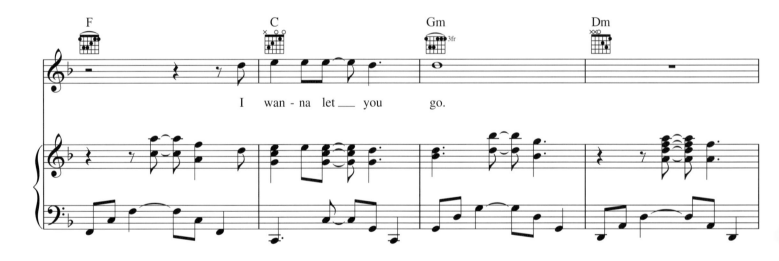

I wan - na let ___ you go.

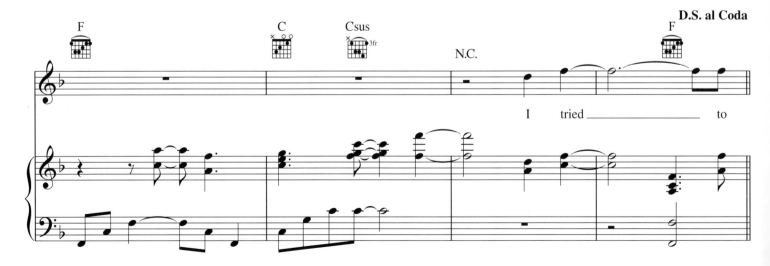

D.S. al Coda

I tried _____ to

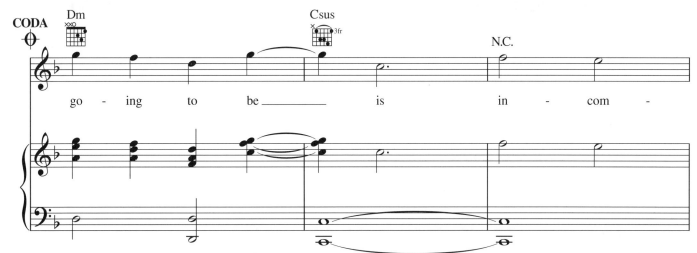

go - ing to be _____ is in - com -

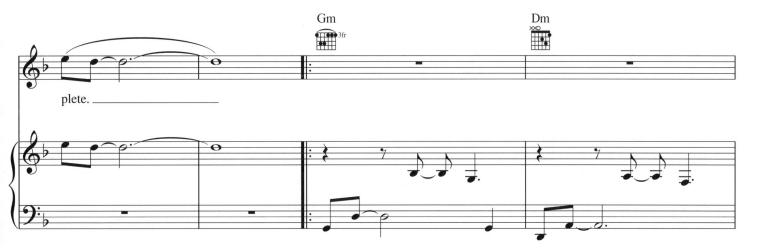

plete. _____

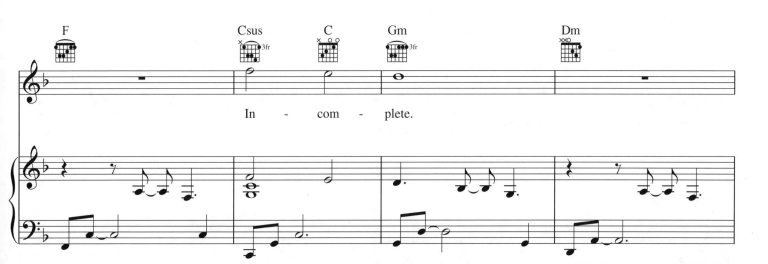

In - com - plete.

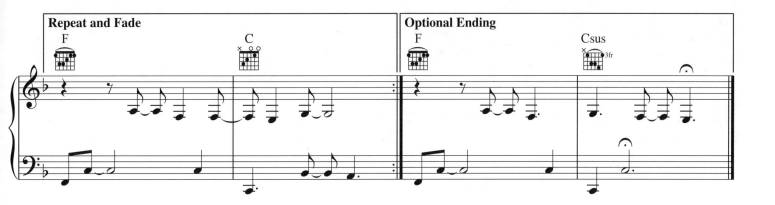

JUST WANT YOU TO KNOW

Words and Music by MARTIN SANDBERG
and LUKASZ GOTTWALD

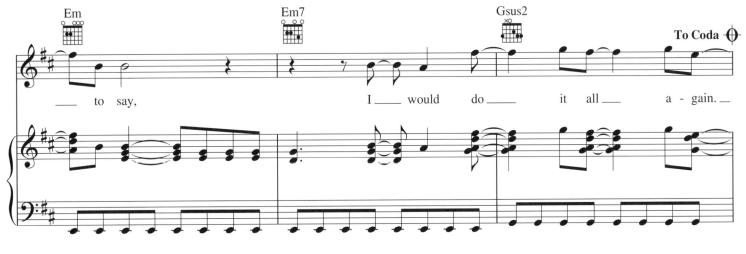

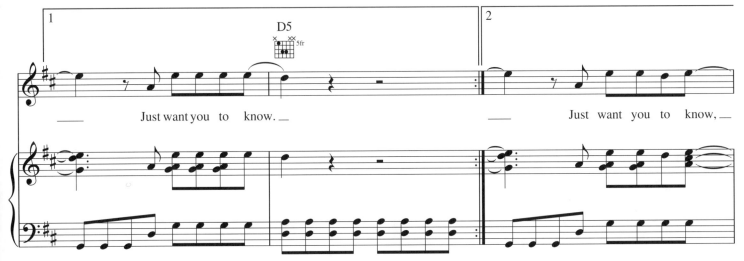

Yes, I just want you to know __

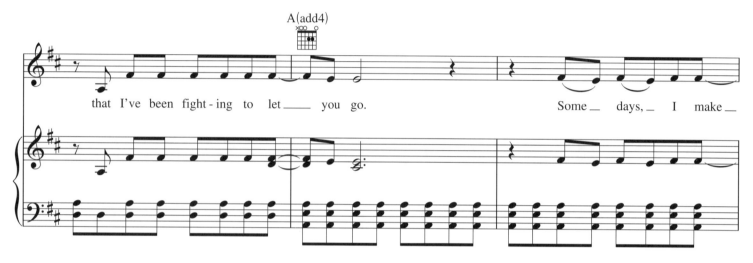

that I've been fight - ing to let __ you go. Some __ days, __ I make __

__ it through, and then __ there's nights __ that nev - er end. __

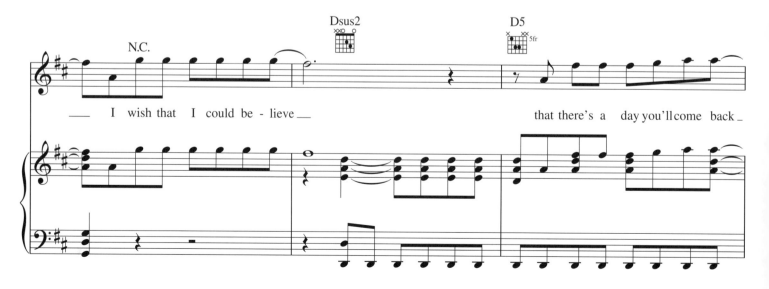

__ I wish that I could be - lieve __ that there's a day you'll come back __

to me. But _ still, _ I have _ to say,

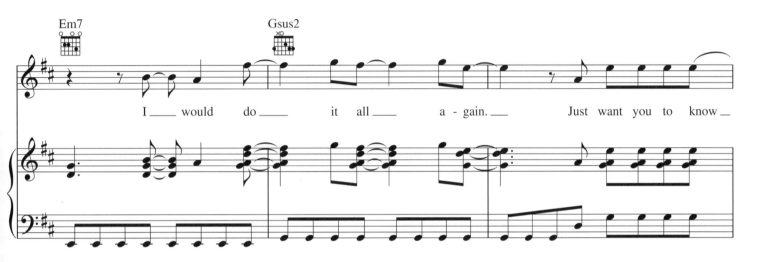

I _ would do _ it all _ a - gain. _ Just want you to know _

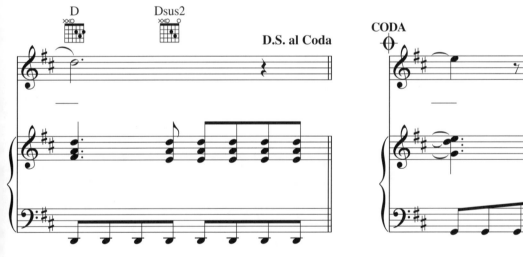

D.S. al Coda

CODA

Just want you to know. _

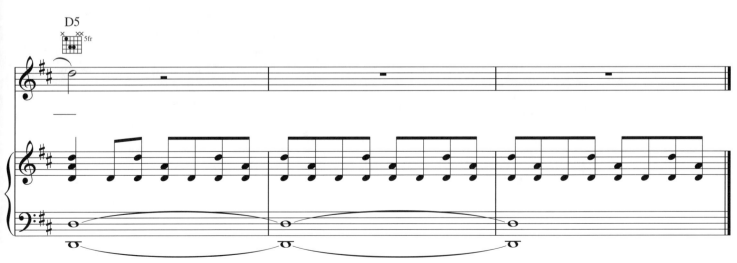

CRAWLING BACK TO YOU

Words and Music by BLAIR DALY
and CHRIS FARREN

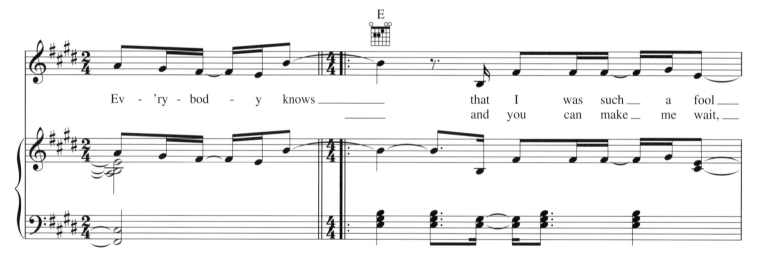

Ev - 'ry - bod - y knows _____ that I was such ___ a fool ___
and you can make ___ me wait, ___

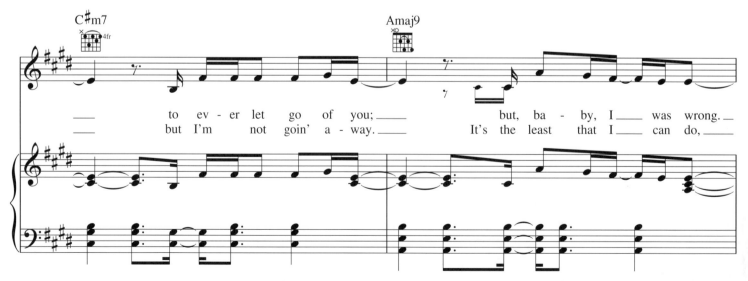

___ to ev - er let go of you; _____ but, ba - by, I ___ was wrong.
___ but I'm not goin' a - way. ___ It's the least that I ___ can do,

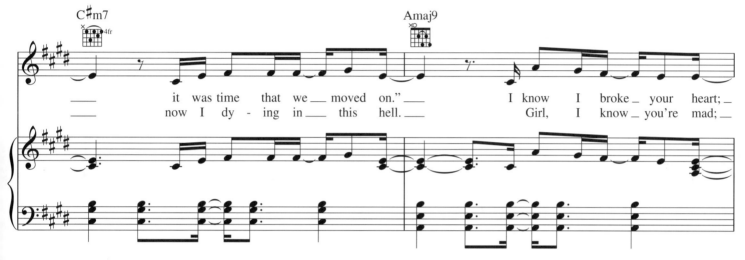

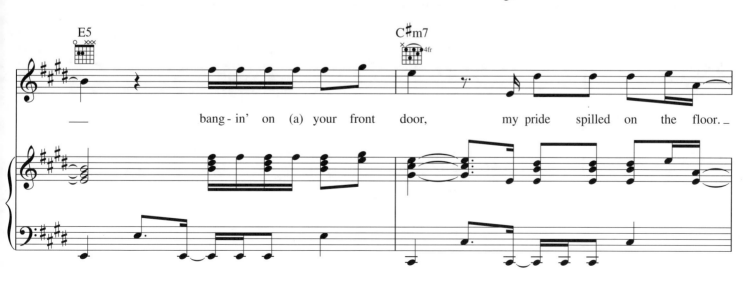

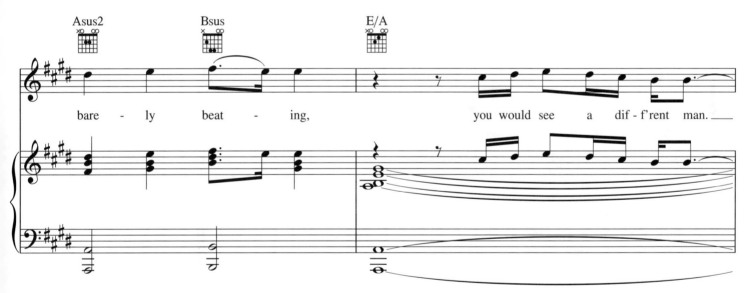

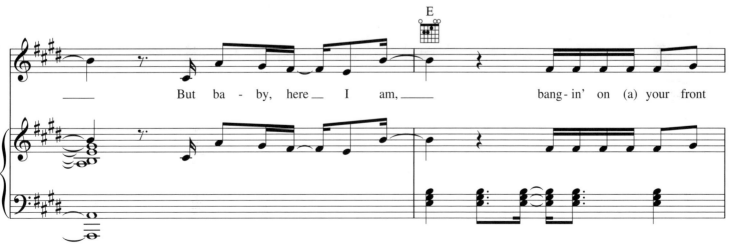

WEIRD WORLD

Words and Music by JOHN ONDRASIK
and GREGG WATTENBERG

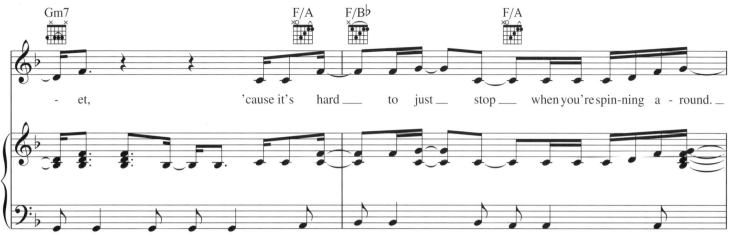

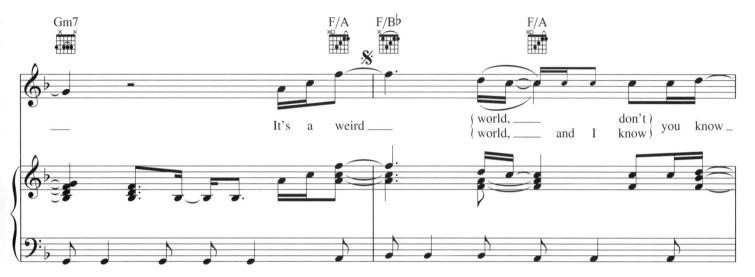

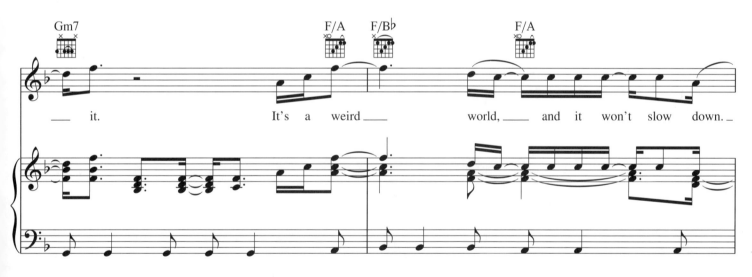

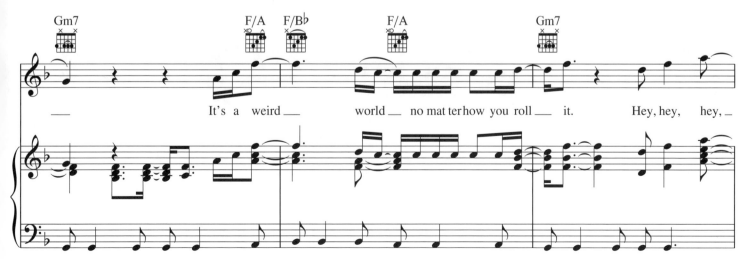

sweet ba - by, there's a way ___ to stand up and fight ___

___ it. Hey, hey, hey, ___ nev-er give up, and don't let it ___ wear out ___ your love. ___

To Coda ⊕

___ It's a weird ___ world, ___

___ yeah. Sent a mes - sage to ___ a G - I in the des - ert; said, "Thank ___

D.S. al Coda

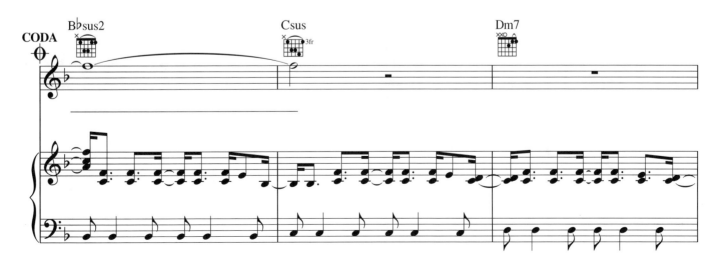

I'm clos-ing my eyes, __ but I'm start-ing to see,

while he's look-ing at you __ she's look-ing at me. __ The on-ly thing it does __ is just keep me a-way __

__ from you. __ Show part of this place, but cheer if I die,

but don't let 'em take __ a-way __ your beau-ti-ful __ smile, __ take a-way __ your

I STILL...

Words and Music by MARTIN SANDBERG
and RAMI YACOUB

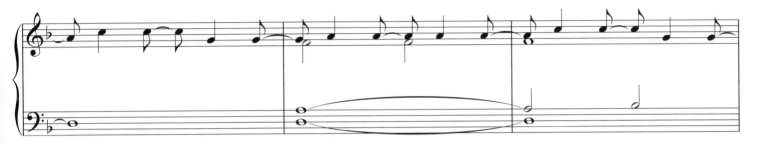

What do _____ you do _____ at this
Now look _____ at me; _____ in-

ver - y mo - ment when _____ I _____ think _____ of _____ you?
stead of mov - ing on, _____ I re - fuse _____ to _____ see _____

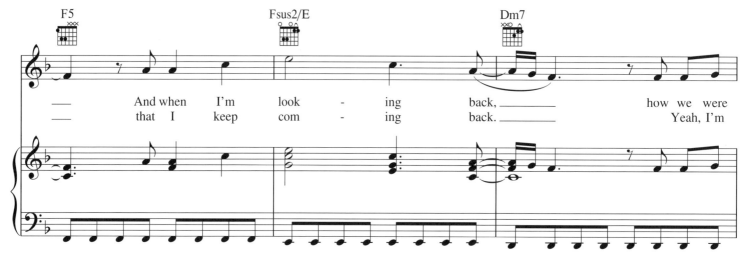

_____ And when I'm look - ing back, _____ how we were
_____ that I keep com - ing back. _____ Yeah, I'm

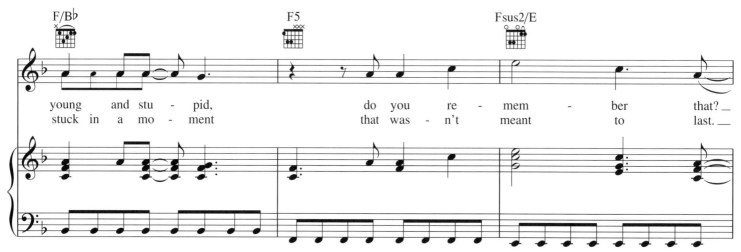

young and stu - pid, do you re - mem - ber that?
stuck in a mo - ment that was - n't meant to last. _____

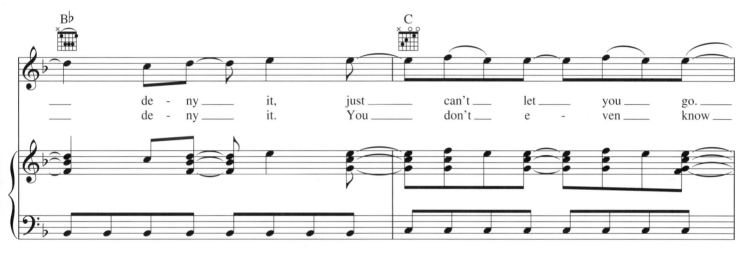

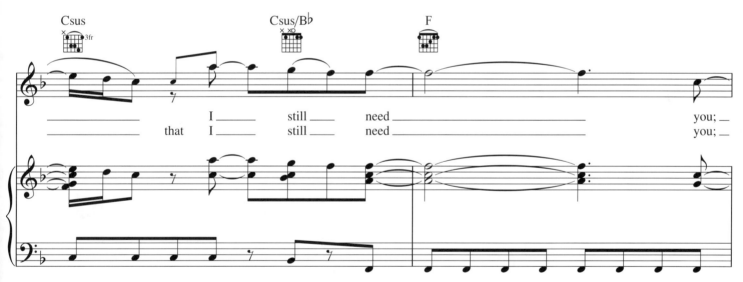

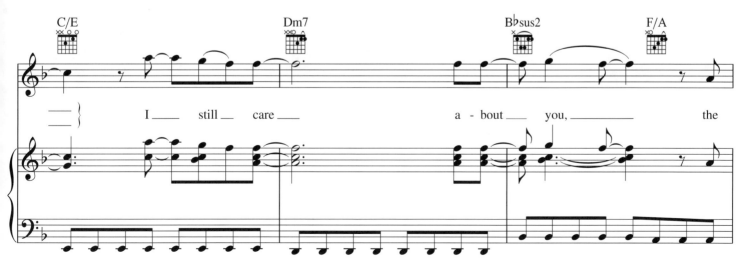

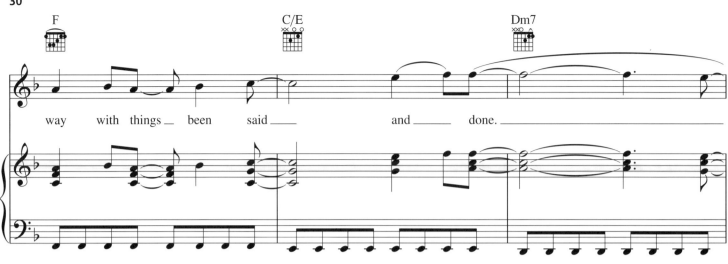

way with things ___ been said ___ and ___ done. ___

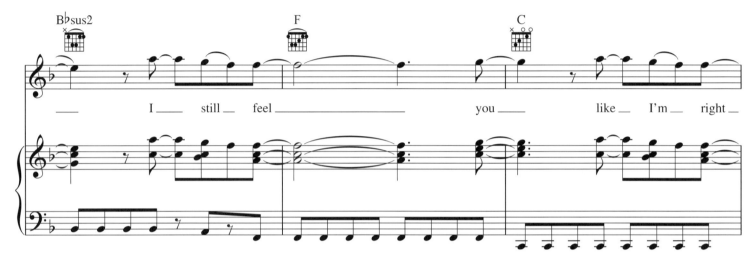

___ I ___ still ___ feel ___ you ___ like ___ I'm ___ right ___

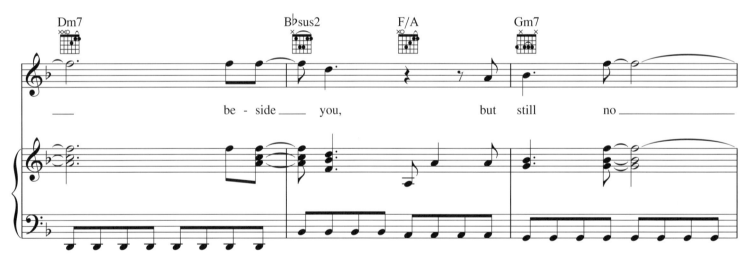

___ be - side ___ you, ___ but still ___ no ___

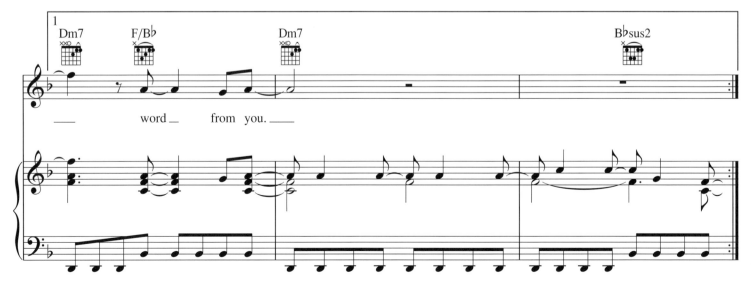

___ word ___ from you. ___

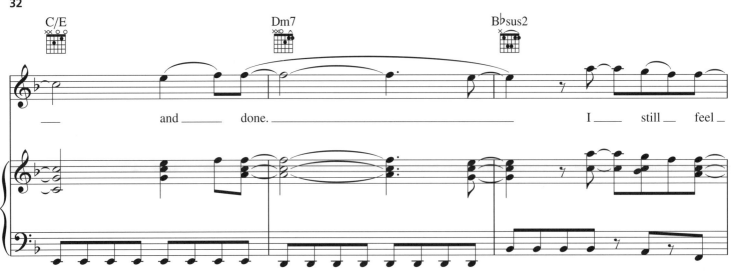

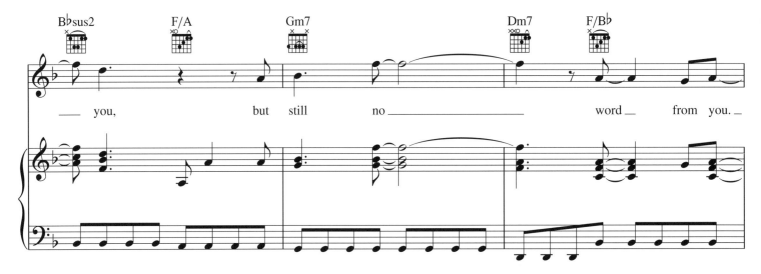

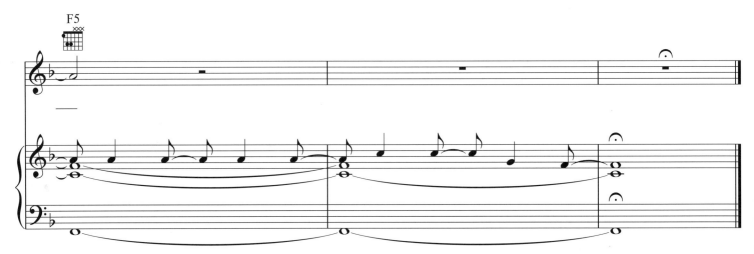

POSTER GIRL

Words and Music by RASMUS BAHNCKE,
RENE TROMBERG and BILLY MANN

la,   la la la   la   la. ___   La la la

la,   la la la   la,   la la la   la   la. ___

Tell me what you want from me;   I've got ev-'ry-thing you need. It's   get-ting hard for me to breathe.

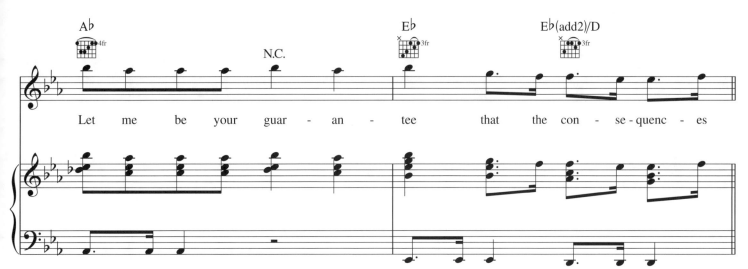

Let me be your guar-an - tee   that the con - se-quenc - es

LOSE IT ALL

Words and Music by WALLY GAGEL,
ALEXANDER FRANCIS BARRY and SHELLY PEIKEN

Play 1st time only

Cm

- ing ___ left. ___
- I've ___ got. ___

Oh. ___

Fm   Gm

I made a prom - ise to ___ my - self last night; ___
If my heart ___ would shat - ter watch - ing you, ___

Fm   Gm

I'm gon - na keep ___ it if ___ it's wrong or right. ___ } And if ___ I
there'd be one ___ less thing ___ I'd have to prove. ___ }

A♭sus2   E♭   B♭

lose it all, ___ there'll be noth - ing left ___ to lose, ___ and I ___ would take ___

CLIMBING THE WALLS

Words and Music by MARTIN SANDBERG
and LUKASZ GOTTWALD

Moderate Rock

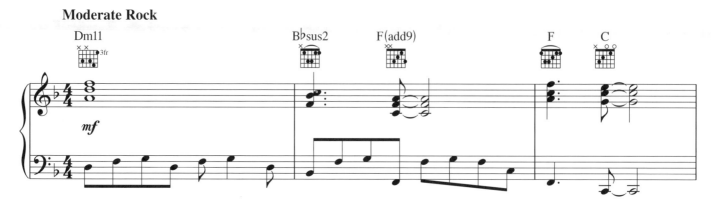

Close your eyes, ___ make a wish ___ and this could last ___
Take my hand, ___ take my life. ___ Just don't take ___

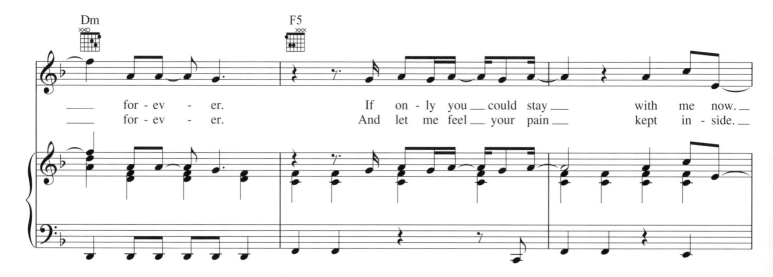

___ for - ev - er. If on - ly you ___ could stay ___ with me now. ___
___ for - ev - er. And let me feel ___ your pain ___ kept in - side.

aah, _____ if I can't have ___ you? ___ It's an il - lu - sion.

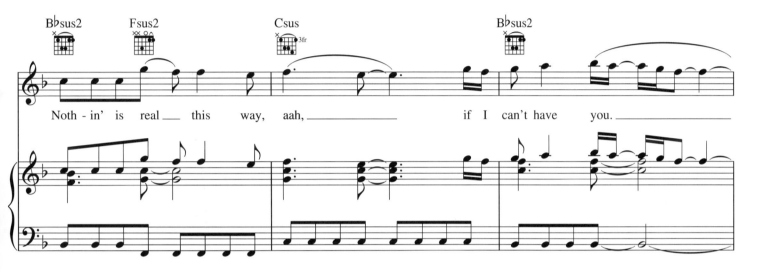

Noth - in' is real ___ this way, aah, _____ if I can't have you. _____

___ No, I can't ___ let ___ you go. ___ You're a

part of me ___ now. Caught by the taste ___ of your kiss. ___ And I

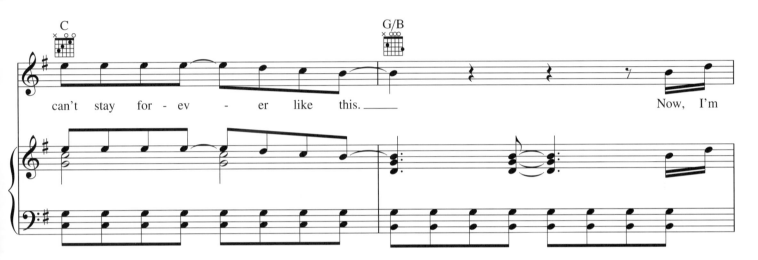

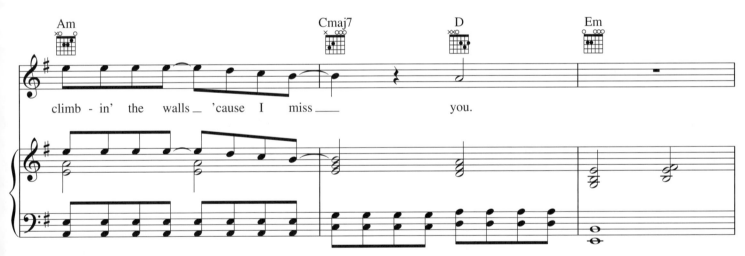

MY BEAUTIFUL WOMAN

Words and Music by PAUL WILTSHIRE
and VICTORIA WU

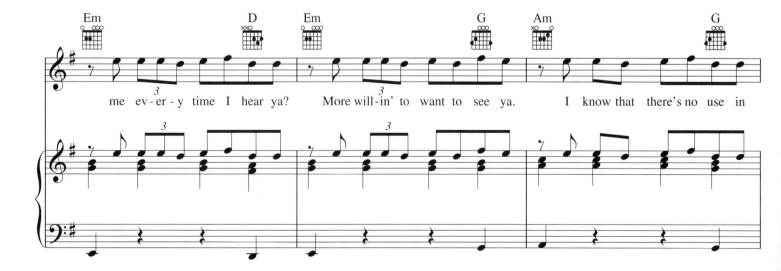

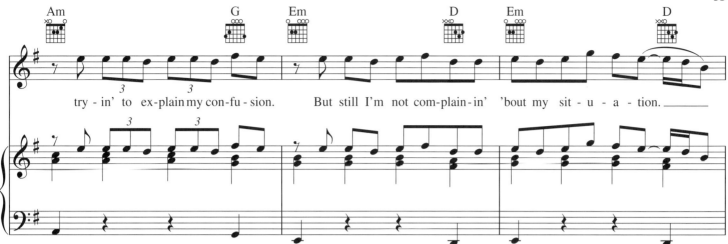

try-in' to ex-plain my con-fu - sion. But still I'm not com-plain-in' 'bout my sit - u - a - tion. _____

Let's not talk a - bout a pos - si - ble end - ing. The ver - y first time that I

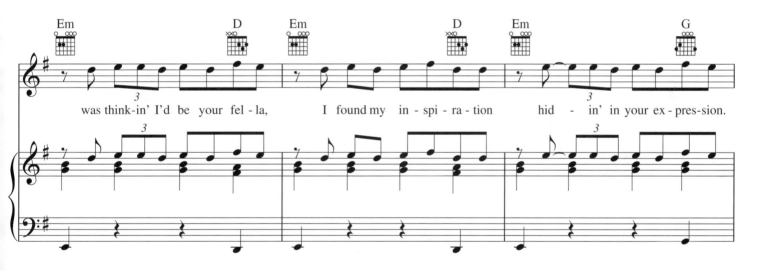

was think-in' I'd be your fel - la, I found my in - spi - ra - tion hid - in' in your ex - pres-sion.

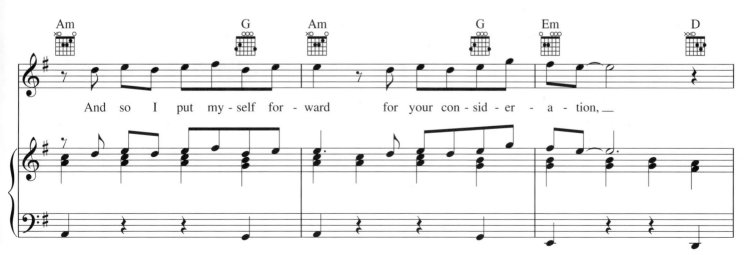

And so I put my - self for - ward for your con - sid - er - a - tion, __

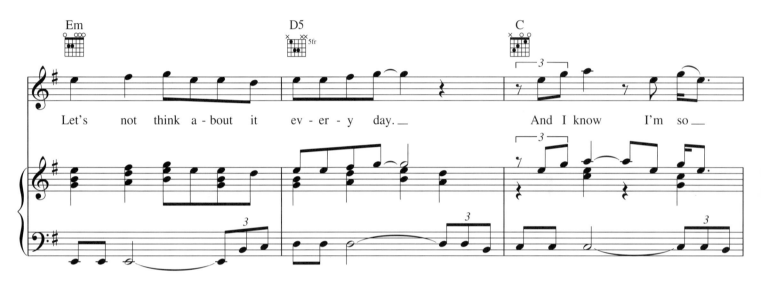

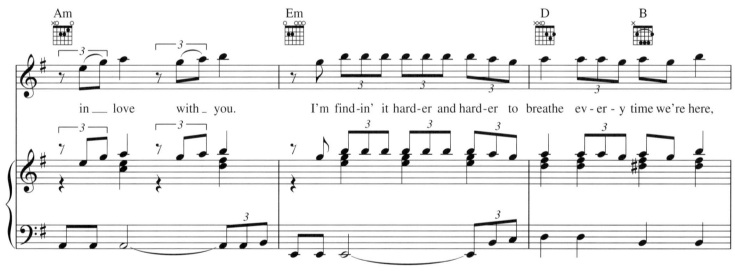

to take you driv-in' down-town. I guess we'll know just what to do __ when you're look-in' to fool a-

Bbm   F/A   Fm/Ab   Eb/G   Gb6   Fm   Eb

round. It's too late to stop me. I know we're gon-na get down. __ Get

Fm   Db   Bbm

down oh no. __ Let's not talk a-bout a pos-si-ble end-ing.

Fm   Eb5   Db

Let's not think a-bout it ev-er-y day. __ And I know I'm so __

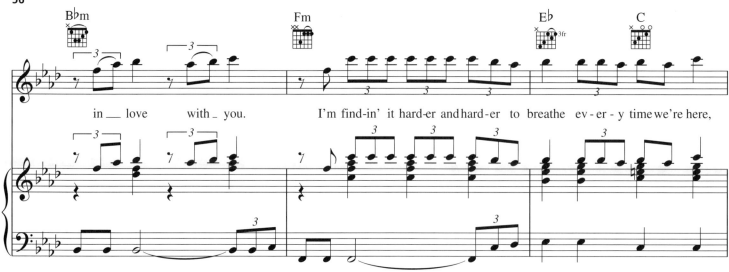

in __ love with _ you. I'm find-in' it hard-er and hard-er to breathe ev - er - y time we're here,

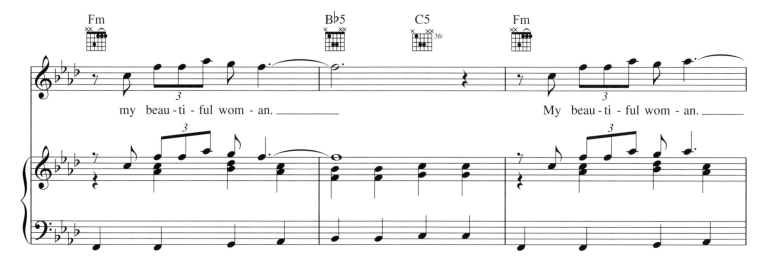

my beau - ti - ful wom - an. _____ My beau - ti - ful wom - an. _____

My beau - ti - ful wom - an. _____

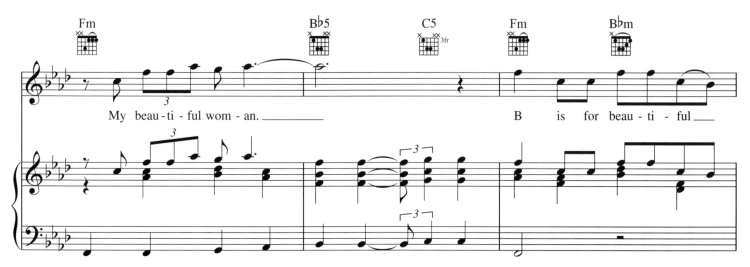

My beau-ti-ful wom - an. _____ B is for beau - ti - ful __

as the sun-shine._ E tells me ev-'ry-thing's_ feel-in' al-right._

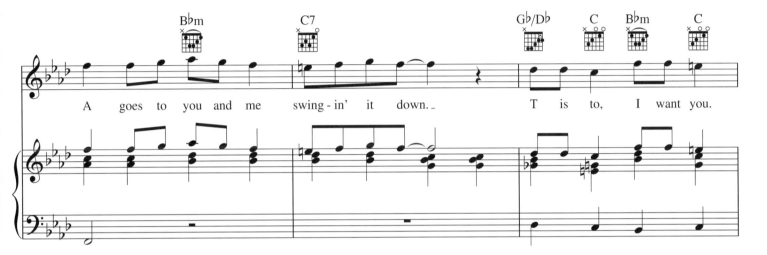

A goes to you and me swing-in' it down._ T is to, I want you.

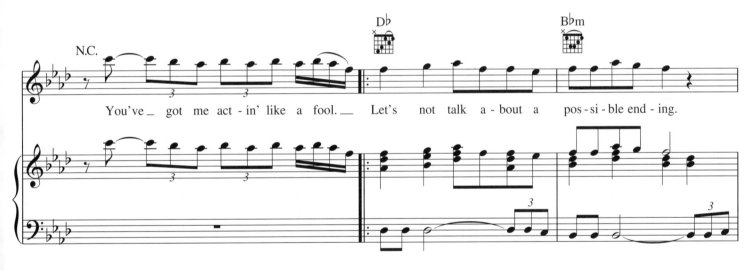

You've_ got me act-in' like a fool._ Let's not talk a-bout a pos-si-ble end-ing.

Let's not think a-bout it ev-er-y day._ And I know I'm so_

SAFEST PLACE TO HIDE

Words and Music by ROBIN LERNER
and TOM LEONARD

Lightly

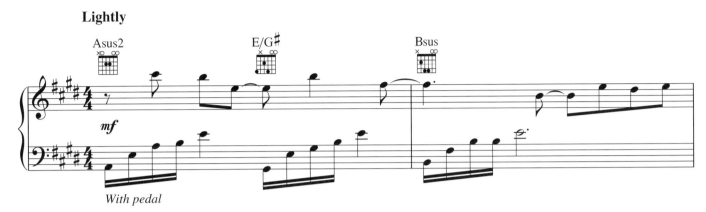

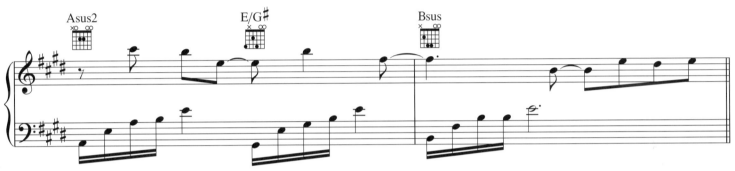

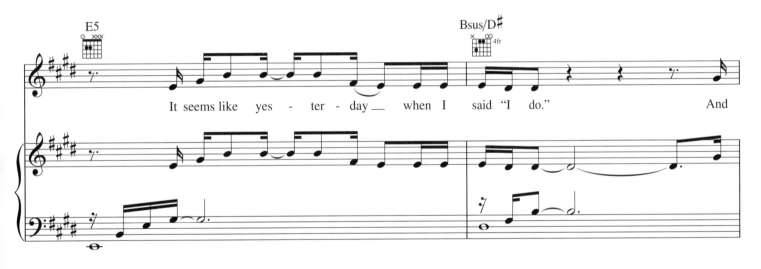

It seems like yes - ter - day __ when I said "I do." __ And

af - ter all __ this time __ my heart __ still burns __ for you. __

If you don't know__ by now__ that you're my on-ly one,__ take a

look in-side__ me and watch my heart__ strings come un-done.__

I know I prom-ised you__ for-ev-er.__

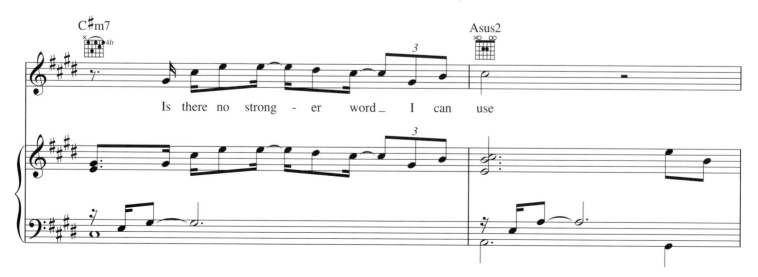

Is there no strong-er word__ I can use

to re-as-sure_ you when_ the storm is rag-ing out - side?_

_____ You're my saf - est place_ to hide. _____ Can you

see me?_ Here_ I am. _____ I

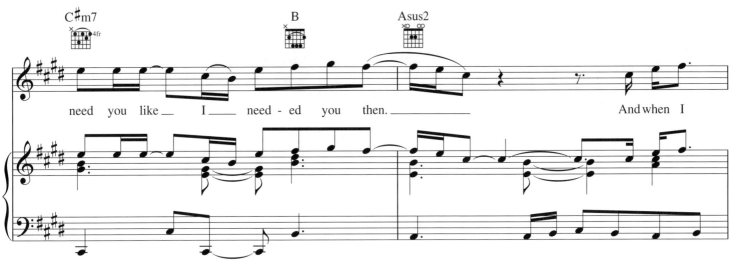

need you like_ I_ need-ed you then. _____ And when I

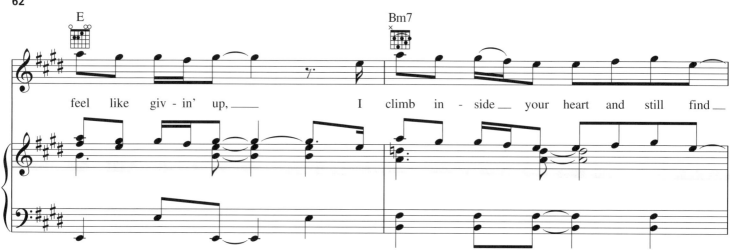

feel like giv - in' up, ____ I climb in - side ____ your heart and still find ____

____ you're my saf - est place ____ to hide. ____

You see col - ors no ____ one else ____ can see.

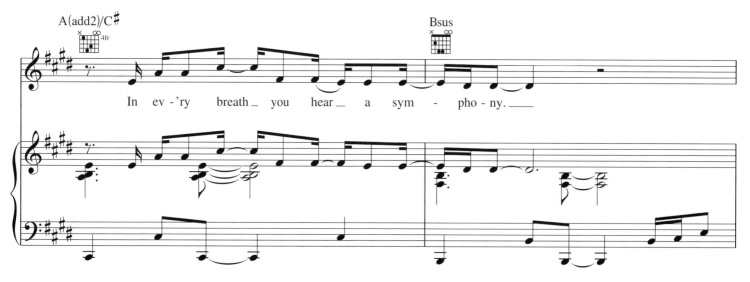

In ev - 'ry breath ____ you hear ____ a sym - pho - ny. ____

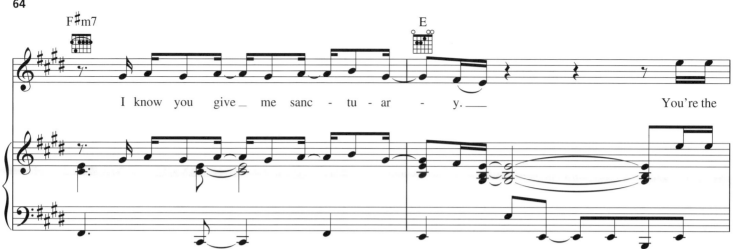

I know you give＿ me sanc - tu - ar - y.＿ You're the

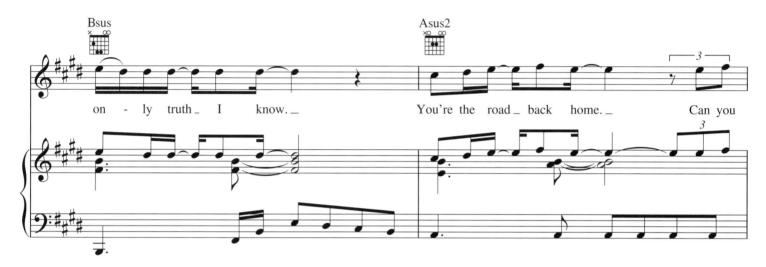

on - ly truth＿ I know.＿ You're the road＿ back home.＿ Can you

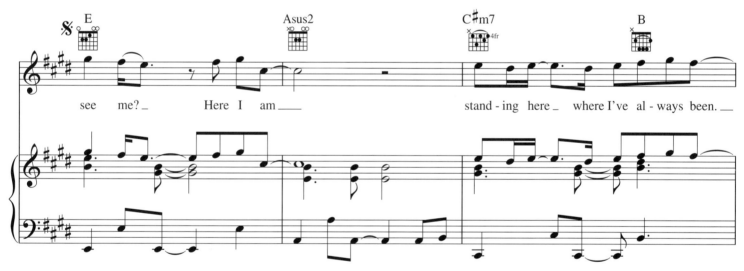

see me?＿ Here I am＿ stand - ing here＿ where I've al - ways been.＿

{ And when words are not e - nough＿ }
{ When I feel like giv - ing up,＿ }　I

climb in - side ___ your heart and still find _____

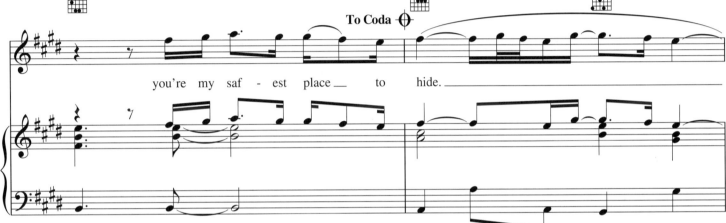

you're my saf - est place ___ to hide. _____

___ My saf - est place ___ to hide.

I know I prom - ised you ___ for - ev - er. ___ There's no strong - er word ___ I

can use to re-as-sure you when the storm is rag-ing out-side.

You're my saf-est place to hide.

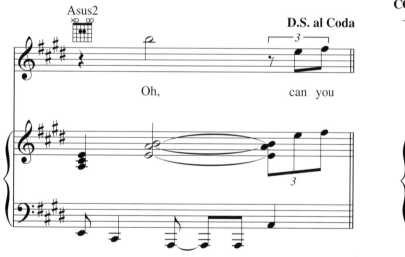

D.S. al Coda

Oh, can you

CODA

hide. Oh yeah,

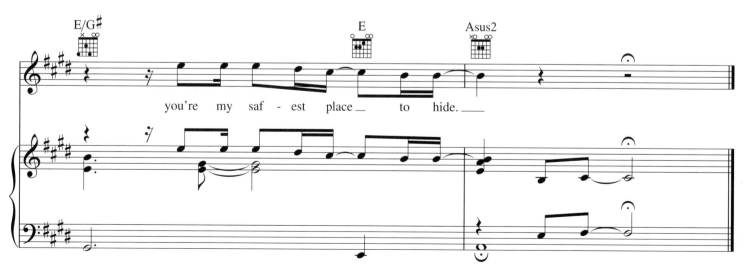

you're my saf-est place to hide.

SIBERIA

Words and Music by MARTIN SANDBERG,
RAMI YACOUB and ALEXANDRA TALOMAA

Moderately

"When you come back __ I won't __ be here," __

she said and gen - tly pulled _ me near. __

"If you wan - na talk __ you __ can call __ and, no, it's not __

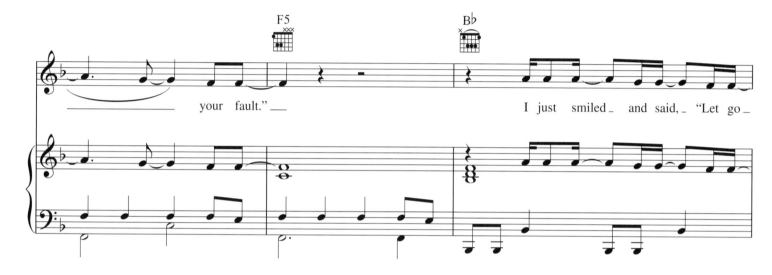

F5   Bb

__ your fault." __   I just smiled _ and said, _ "Let go _

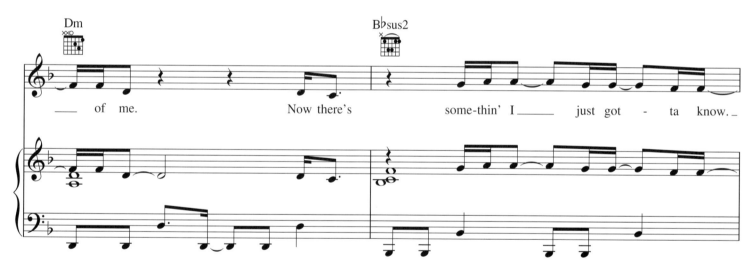

Dm   Bbsus2

__ of me.   Now there's   some - thin' I _____ just got - ta know. _

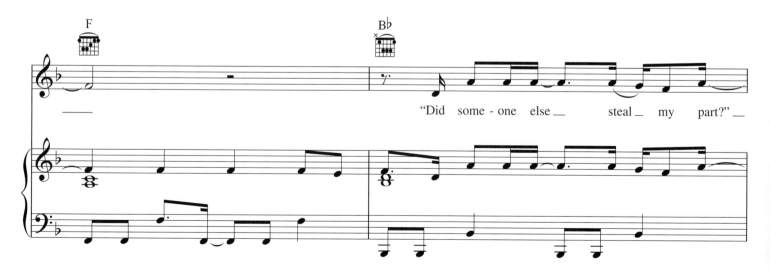

F   Bb

__   "Did some - one else _ steal _ my part?" _

She said, "It's not _____ my fault." _ Then _ my

heart did time in Si - be - ri - a, _____ was wait-in' for the lie to come

true. 'Cause _ it's all so dark and mys - ter - i - ous _____

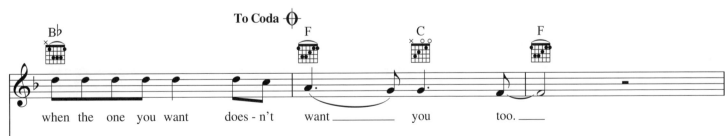

To Coda ⊕

when the one you want does-n't want _____ you too. _____

want you. Gave my-self_ a - way_ com-plete - ly

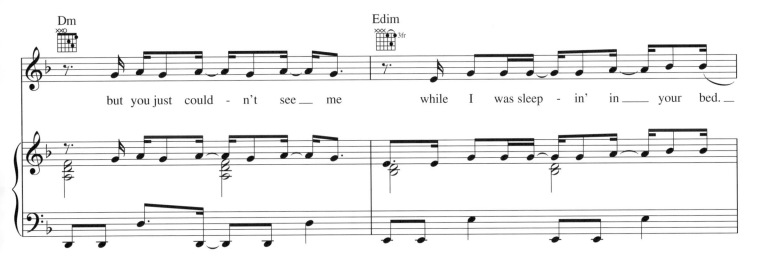

but you just could - n't see _ me while I was sleep - in' in _ your bed. _

_ 'Cause some - one else_ was on _ your

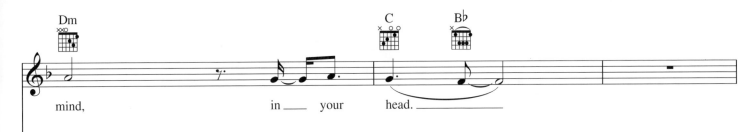

mind, in _ your head. _

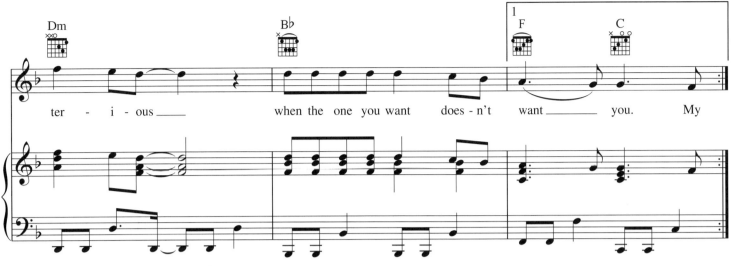

ter - i - ous ___ when the one you want does-n't want ___ you. My

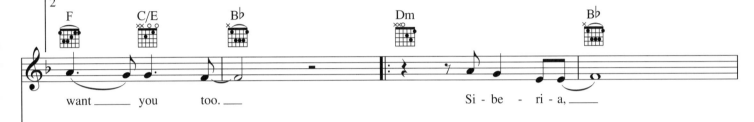

want ___ you too. ___ Si - be - ri - a, ___

Si - be - ri - a. ___

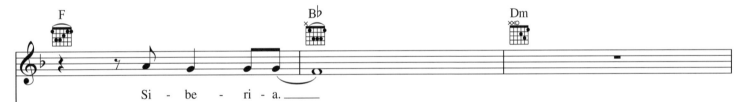

Optional Ending

Repeat and Fade

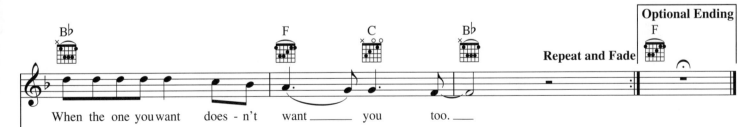

When the one you want does-n't want ___ you too. ___

NEVER GONE

Words and Music by KEVIN RICHARDSON,
GARY BAKER and STEVE DIAMOND

Moderately, in 2

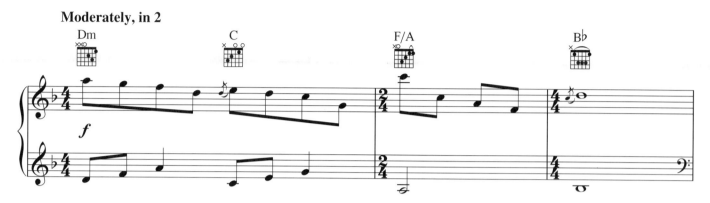

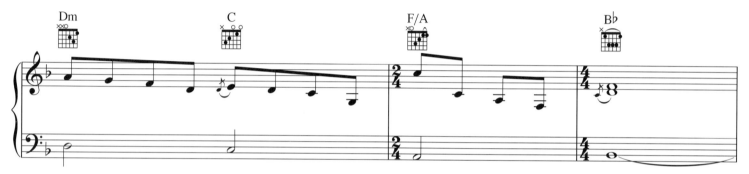

The things we did.___ The things we said ___ keep
walk a - long ___ these emp - ty streets, ___

com - in' back to me and make me ___ smile a - gain. ___ You showed me how ___ to
there is not a sec - ond you're not ___ here with me. The love you gave, ___ the

face the truth. ___ Ev-'ry-thing that's good in me, I owe to you. ___
grace you showed ___ will al-ways be my strength and be my cor - ner stone. ___

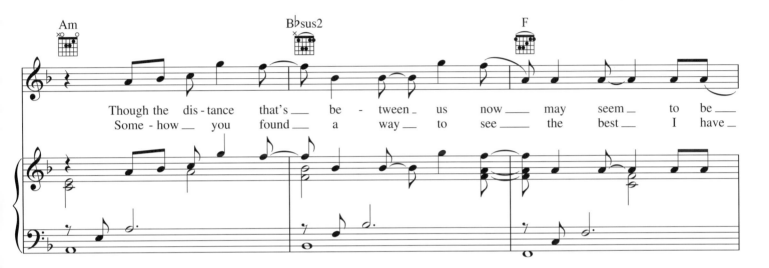

Though the dis - tance that's ___ be - tween us now ___ may seem ___ to be ___
Some - how ___ you found ___ a way ___ to see ___ the best ___ I have ___

___ too far, ___ it will nev - er sep - ar - ate ___ us.
___ in me. ___ As long ___ as time ___ goes on, ___ I

Deep in - side ___ I know ___ you are ___ nev - er gone, ___
swear to you ___ that you ___ will be ___

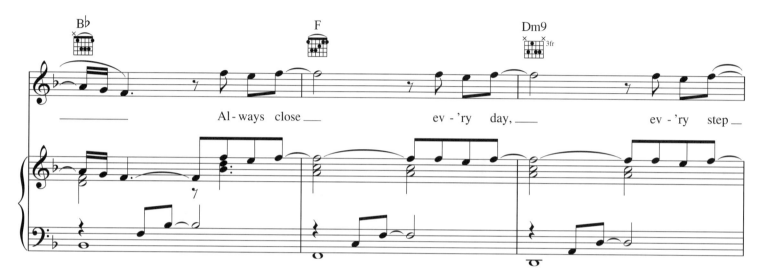

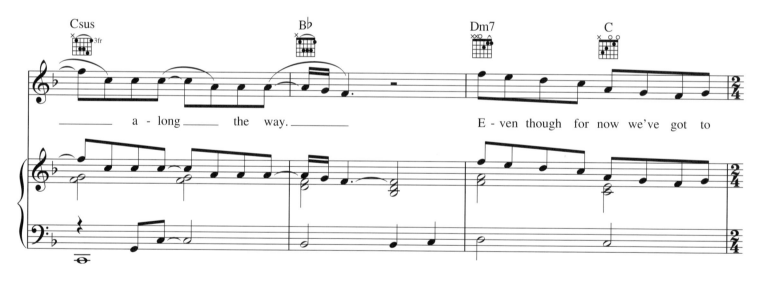

Nev - er gone. _____

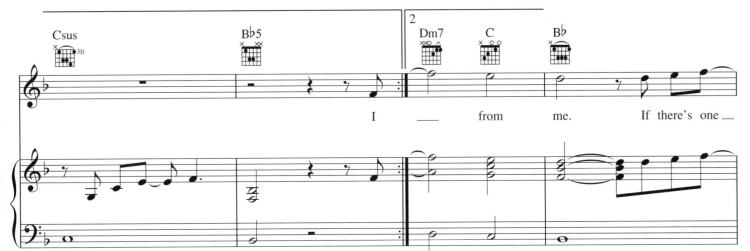

I ___ from me. If there's one ___

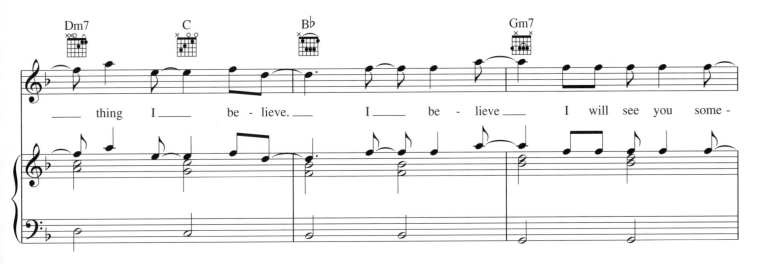

___ thing I ___ be - lieve. ___ I ___ be - lieve ___ I will see you some -

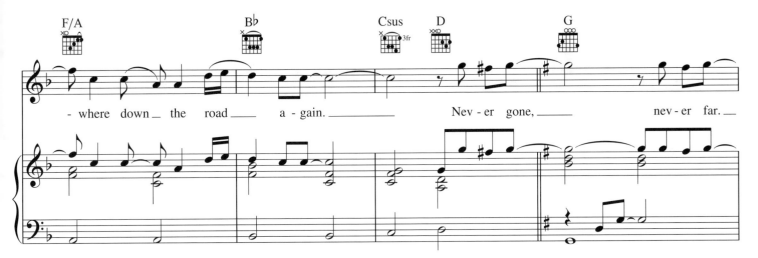

- where down ___ the road ___ a - gain. _____ Nev - er gone, _____ nev - er far. ___

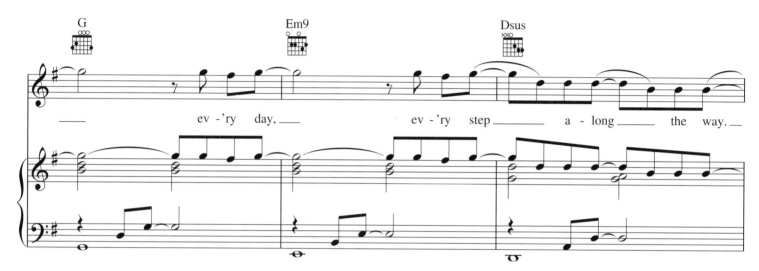

Nev - er gone, _____ nev - er far. _____ In my heart _____

_____ is where _____ you are. _____ Al - ways close _____ ev - 'ry day, _____

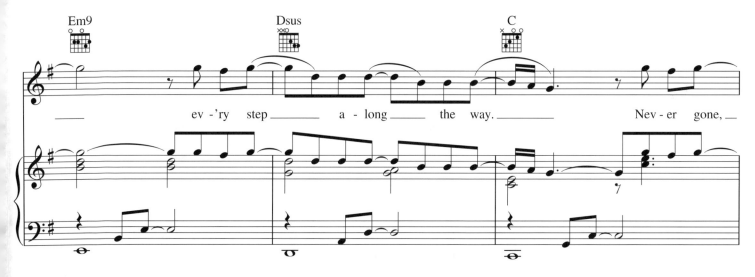

ev - 'ry step _____ a - long _____ the way. _____ Nev - er gone, _____

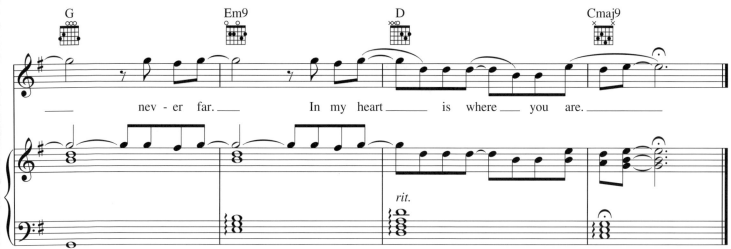

_____ nev - er far. _____ In my heart _____ is where _____ you are. _____